Strathyre
Balquhidder
Lochearnhead
In
Old Photographs

compiled by
Ewen W. Cameron, O.B.E.

Stirling District Libraries
1994

Stirling
DISTRICT COUNCIL

© Stirling District Libraries
1994

ISBN 1 870542 28 2

Compiled by
Ewen Cameron O.B.E.

Printed by
Cordfall Ltd
041 332 4640

Ewen Cameron throwing the hammer in 1953, the year he became Scottish Champion.

The judge is one of the famous family of Nicholsons from Tighnabruich who were great shinty players and could raise a full family team.

Cover illustrations   Front Cover: Main road from Callander into Lochearnhead before the 1914 / 18 war.

                                               Back Cover: The east end of Strathyre, 1895.

This small offering is for both the young and the old of our district and I hope you will all enjoy it. I wish I had space for all the photographs that came my way; the hardest part of all was "cutting down".

ACKNOWLEDGEMENTS:

To my wife Anne, and to Kay Riddell for all their help and patience.

Thanks also to so many others who kept my enthusiasm going and in particular to Ronnie Hamilton, Bunty MacDonald and Jock Innes of Strathyre; Jeananne MacNaughton and Mrs Jill Love of Balquhidder; and Andrew Dow, Hugh MacDiarmid, Mary Kennedy-Mathieson, Cathie Kennedy and Stan Collingwood of Lochearnhead.

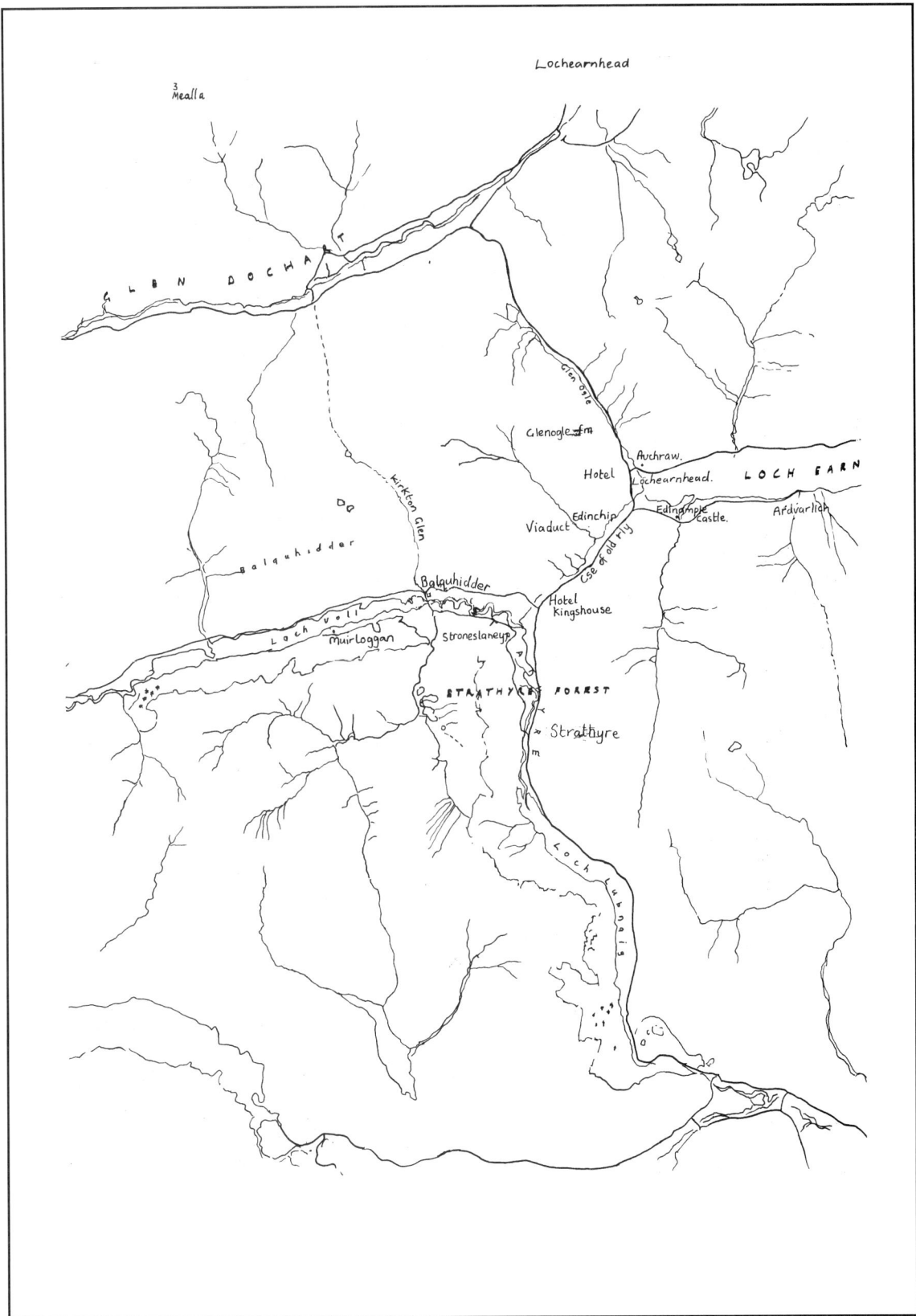

Lochearnhead

3
Meall a

GLEN DOCHART

Glen Ogle

Glenogle Fm

Auchraw.

Hotel

Lochearnhead.

LOCH EARN

Kirkton Glen

Balquhidder

Edinchip

Viaduct

Edinample
Castle.

Ardvorlich

Cse of old Rly

Balquhidder

Hotel
Kingshouse

Loch Voil

Muirloggan

Stroneslaney

STRATHYRE FOREST

Strathyre

Loch Lubnaig

STRATHYRE

A view of the west end of Strathyre around 1895.

Opposite top
   The west end of the main road, Strathyre, 1895.

Opposite below
   The east end of Strathyre from the site of the Strathyre Inn. 1895

The Street, Strathyre.

The Old Meal Mill, c1930.

This is no longer but was on the back road to Balquhidder

A group of workers building Strathyre station around 1870.

The building was destroyed by fire in 1893 and then rebuilt.

Opposite.
Strathyre Station in all its glory, 1900.

As many of us still remember it, rebuilt after the fire. When the line opened from Oban to Callander, Glasgow and Edinburgh there were seven trains each way in the summer and four in the winter. Change at Stirling for Edinburgh. The trip from Balquhidder to Glasgow Buchanan Street took two hours. The train was always warm and their was a restaurant car with full High Tea with all the trimmings which got into Balquhidder at 18.50. The "milk train" got you home by 01.00 after an evening in Town. In the years 1992 / 93 the site of the station has been developed by Scottish Homes – and very nice too.

Black Watch Reserve Territorials 1936
Extreme left: Jock Innes of Strathyre and second from right Donald Fraser of Lochearnhead. Donald became a regular soldier with the rank of sergeant but lost a leg during the War. Four male Frasers and sister Jean all served in the Forces.

The War Memorial in Strathyre, c1920

Inside Strathyre Church, in 1904.
This closed as did Lochearnhead Church of Scotland about 1982, and Balquhidder is now the only church of this denomination left in the area. Services are now held there and in the St. Angus Episcopal Church, Lochearnhead.

The retiral of the Rev. Roy Rigg from the parish in 1973.
Left to right—
Back row: Davie MacDiarmid, Mary Cairney, Andrew Dow
Sitting: Mrs Rigg, Don Ferguson, Auntie Meg Fergusson and Rev, Rigg.
A very popular Minister.

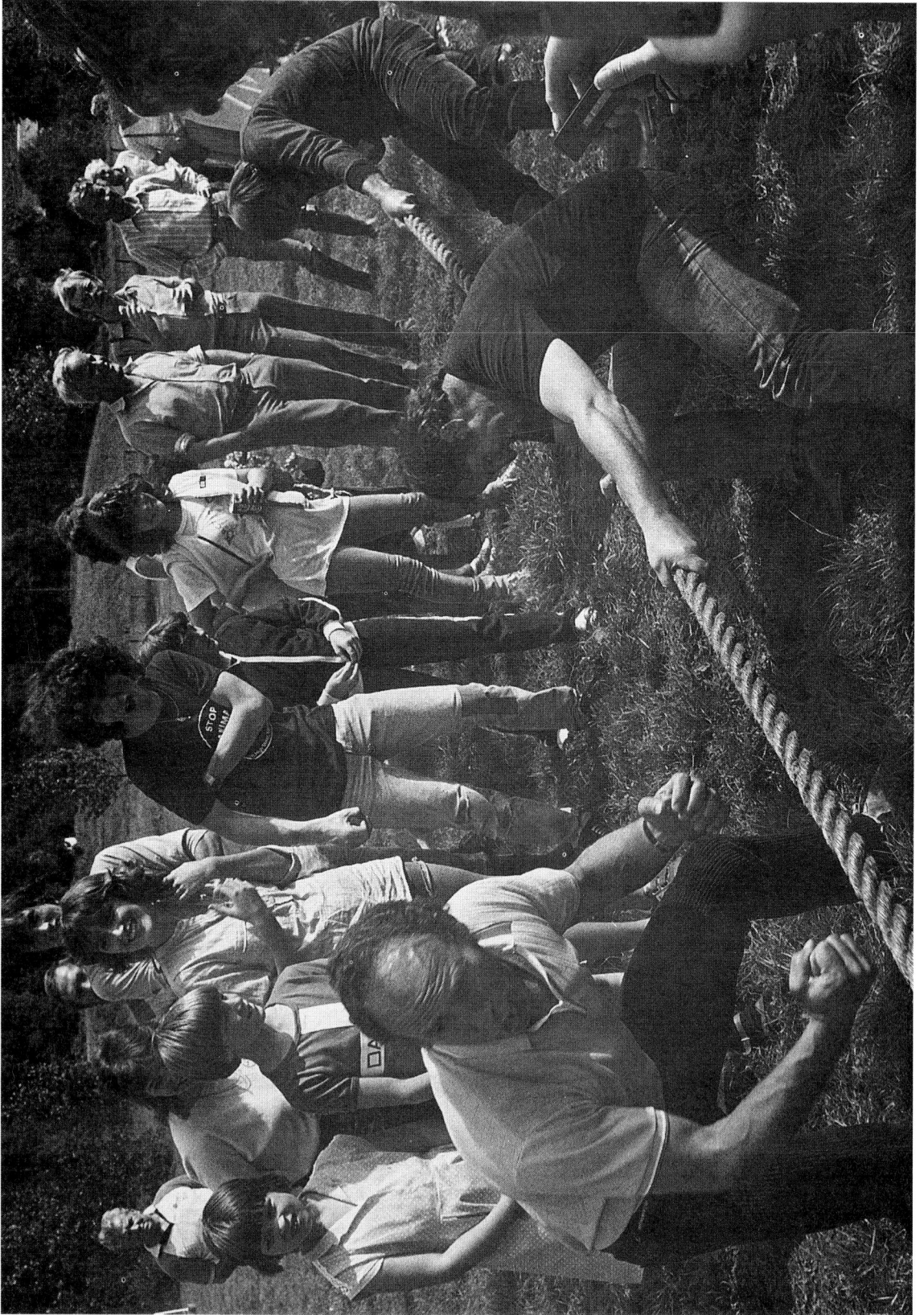

Opposite
Strathyre Fete, 1981, with the Ben Sheann tug-o-war team
    Included in the picture are—
Leigh Ferguson, Calum Falconer, Kenny Wills, Alison
McAlister, Crawford Cook, Alaina Cook, Roger Sharp,
Ronnie Hamilton and Fiona Perks.

Three generations of weavers mid 19th century.
    Thought to be outside Stronslaney on the back road
to Balquhidder

BALQUHIDDER

Spinning Granny, Mrs Fergusson, Blaircreich, mid 19th century.
    Grandmother of J.C. Fergusson and Great Grandmother of Don and Ethne who still uses this wheel.

Opposite
The Balquhidder Church from the Kirkton Burn and the Old Bridge c1890

Mr and Mrs (John and Margaret) MacNaughton, Inverlochlarig, in 1896

Opposite above
Kingshouse Halt.

This was erected by the people of the glen by public subscription and the name became Kingshouse in July 1931. Stops were by request and many a sleeping shepherd was wakened up in Oban after a "guid day" at the sales in Stirling! By tradition they were given a free run back down the line at 0600 hours the following morning.

Opposite below
The Post Office at Balquhidder Station.

When the line opened to Oban this was called Lochearnhead Station but the name changed to Balquhidder when the branch line to Lochearnhead and Crieff opened in 1904, and another station was built at Lochearnhead. This is now the Golden Larches Restaurant

A ploughing match at Tulloch, 1912.

On the left are Mr Fergusson of Tulloch and Mr Fisher of Balliemore.

Kirkton Farm, Balquhidder, 1930.

One of the very few times that the games were held in Balquhidder. The local country dance team with piper Hugh MacDiarmid senior, a master mason in Lochearnhead.

Balquhidder Games, 1937.

Lady MacGregor of MacGregor, wife of Sir Malcolm handing over the cup for the local heavyweight events to Champion Donald MacKillop of Stronvar.

The first car to drive across the ford to the top of Balquhidder. Miss Jean MacNaughton and friends.

Summer of 1932.

Two old gentlemen, Grandfather John MacNaughton and his brother Duncan, on a day's outing to Killin Show.

Mrs Tom Waters with her daughters Ada and Sheena outside Edinample Castle, 1917.

Miss Ada is pictured elsewhere in this book and her sister, Miss Sheena, became a doctor and only returned to the area to retire. She lived at Edinample until she died in the late 80s.

Photographed in 1925, three generations of blacksmiths in Balquhidder, left to right, father Duncan, the smith and local Registrar, his son Alister who did not follow the trade and grandfather Sandy MacNaughton.

Mr and Mrs Watters Macrae of Edinample Castle at a Balquhidder wedding, 1949.

Mr and Mrs Sim Ballingal, Ardveich at a Balquhidder wedding, 1949.

Opposite top, Balquhidder School 1933 / 34.
Back row: Tom Smillie, Alasdair McNaughton, Douglas Stewart, Hamish Smillie,
Bobby Stewart.
Middle row: Margaret Christie, Margaret McNaughton, Elise Christie, Betty Smillie,
Chrissie McRae, Mary Moyes, Rena Moyes, Bunty Haggart, Ethne Fergusson, Morag McRae,
Mary Hamilton, Jean McRae.
Seated: Don Fergusson, James McGeorge, Duncan Stewart, Pat Fergusson (Mid Auchleskine),
Lex Christie, Henry Chambers, Pat Fergusson (Auchleskine).

Opposite lower, Balquhidder School, 1962.
Back row: Margaret Massie, Catherine McVicar, Teresa Matyjasek, Helen Renshaw,
Gillian Perks, Moira Fergusson, Joy Robertson.
Second row: Miss Stewart, Tommy Haig, Walter Anderson, David Thow, Quintus Renshaw,
Robert Allison, Ewen MacGregor, William Massie, Andrew Matyjasek, Mrs Beauchamp.
Third row: Douglas McVicar, Fiona Shepherd, Alaine Mitchell, Ailsa Anderson,
Margaret McDiarmid, Betty Massie, Patricia Haig, Leslie Massie, - Jackson.
Front row: . . ., . . ., Martin Mitchell, Catriona ?, Sandra Shepherd, Duncan McDiarmid,
John McVicar, James Jackson.

Below, Balquhidder School, 1970.
Back row: Carolyn McNaughton, Duncan McDiarmid, Grace Stewart, Kirk Gauld,
Christine McDiarmid.
Middle row: Colin McDiarmid, Claire Bain, Forbes Gauld, James Jackson, Penny Thomson,
Robert Ferguson, Mrs Beauchamp
Front row: Alison Clark, Gavin Keir, Frances Cocker, Fiona MacNaughton,
Stewart Fergusson.

Strolling toward the Kirkton Glen in 1945.
Left to right: Jimmy Stewart, Gregor MacGregor and Duncan Stewart,

Balquhidder girl Heather Love marries Alastair Gilchrist from Strathyre in 1949.

The groom joined the navy as a "boy" and on his sad and sudden death had reached the rank of Vice Admiral.

Opposite
Making the film *The 39 Steps* in Balquhidder, 1959.

Kenneth Moore chatting to the "extras": Jimmy Stewart, John Ferguson, Stevie Sinclair, Peter Grant and unidentified.

The Rev David Cameron and Mrs Cameron. Minister of the parish some thirty years. With him outside the Inn are the Misses Baillie-Hamilton.

Alastair and Anne MacNaughton who farmed the Braes for thirtysix years until 1978

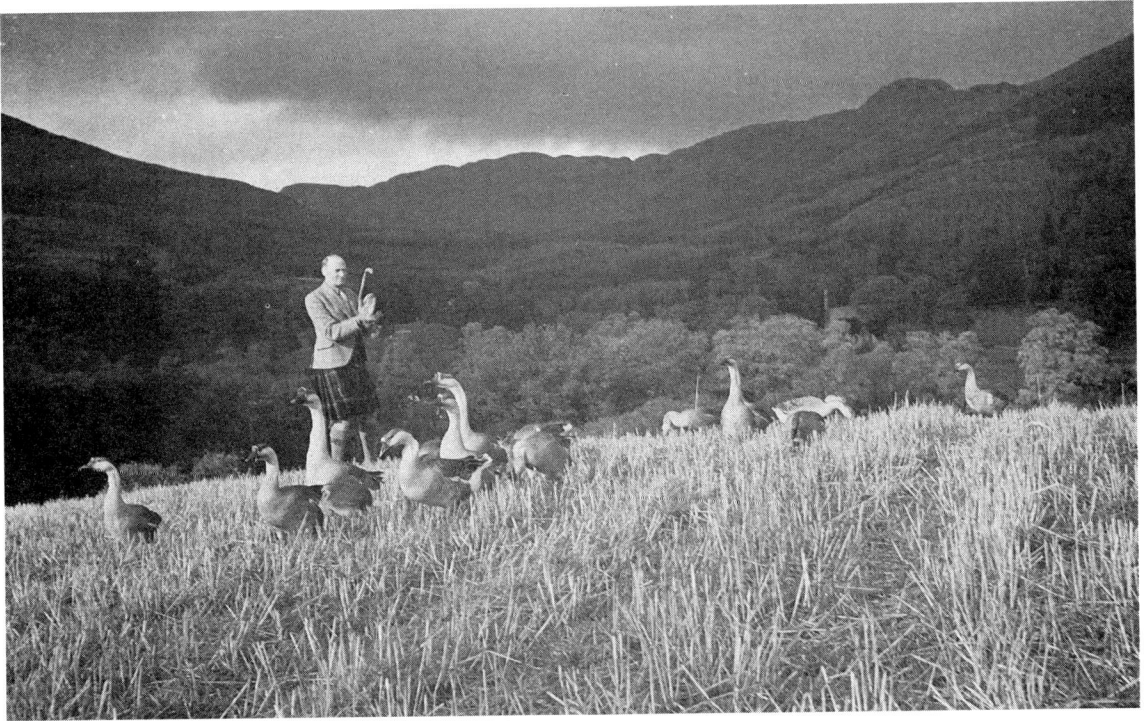

Colonel Geoffrey Stuart Love tending his geese with Kirkton Glen behind him. The Love family retired to Tigh na Croit after the War.

During his parliamentary campaign in 1963 the then Lord Home with Ian MacVicar at the latter's home, *Immerion* in Balquhidder. On winning the election Lord Home became Prime Minister and left the House of Lords for the Commons.

An art exhibition in the Balquhidder Hall, 1980.
Left to right: Betty Beauchamp, Kitty MacLachlan of Lochearnhead Post Office and Mary malcolm.

The last gathering of Blaircreich Hills in September 1985, before the Forestry took over.

Don Fergusson, Duncan Stewart, Stewart Fergusson, Colin McDiarmid, Davie McDiarmid, Andrew Key, Tom Lambie.

Mr John McNaughton, Inverlochlarig receiving his O.B.E. at the Palace, with his wife Jeananne and his sons Malcolm and Allan.

LOCHEARNHEAD

Above
A view of Auchraw from Ravenscroft, c1880.

In left foreground is the old Lochearnhead Inn, in use until 1746 when the Lochearnhead Hotel was built for use by General Wade's troops during the time of the road building through Glenogle.

Opposite top
Main road into Lochearnhead from Callander before the 1914 / 18 war.

Opposite below
Glenogle, 1885.

On the left the railway is nearly completed, the General Wade road (1746 / 47 in the middle and the "new" main road on the right. Beside the right hand bend on the Wade road, by this time grass, a house can just be seen. It is thought that this house must have been for the use of engineers during the building of the railway. As this picture has lain in an old album in Ogle Park for over a century no-one in the village has seen this house before.

The opening of the line to Crieff and Gleneagles, 1904.

A passenger train going over the viaduct eastwards to St Fillans. The ruin on the left is the old Lochearnhead Inn.

Opposite
Lochearnhead station ready for opening day, 1904.

A train crossing the viaduct on the lower line, with Edinchip House in the background.

Opposite
Lochearnhead Church in 1904 as seen from the South Lochearn Road. In the background is the viaduct over the Balquhidder / Lochearnhead line on the Edinchip Estate.

Goods traffic at the newly opened station, 1905.

The left hand line is the main track. The beech wood in the distance went 1800 feet to the top of the hill but was felled during the Great War for timber. The lower trees are still there. The house in the foreground is View Cottage, then the home of Hugh MacDiarmid the local stonemason whose son Hugh was headmaster of a Perth school, and a great help with the publication of this book.

LOCHEARNHEAD. STATION. T.U.SUL. O.W.W.

The old Lochearnhead Hotel in 1892
owned by Mr Maisey.

Mrs Chrissie Cameron has just taken over the hotel from her mother, Mrs Maben, 1922.

These ladies are the grandmother and mother of the three Cameron children Margaret, Ailie and Ewen.

The staff of Lochearnhead Hotel in 1905. Front row is the dairy maid holding a pet lamb. This is Mrs Kennedy who became the mother of the twelve Kennedys in Glenogle living in the croft for over sixty years.

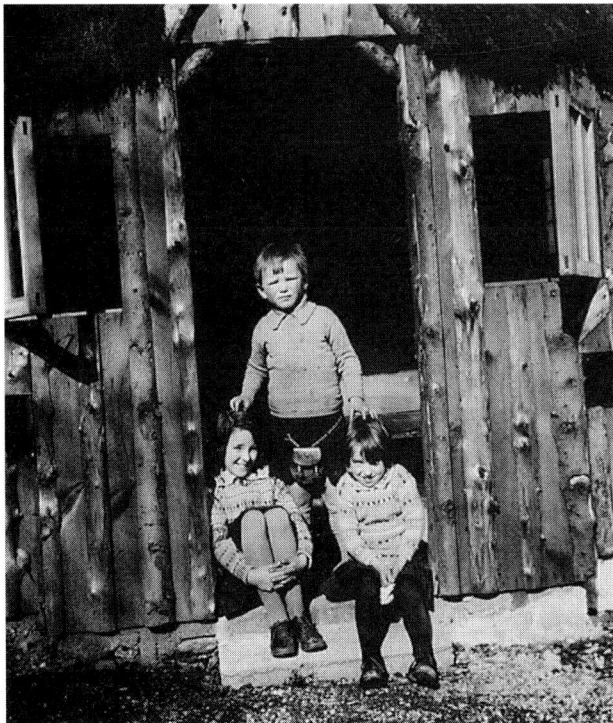

The Cameron children whose grandmother, Mrs Maben (nee McCrae) took over the hotel in 1916 and whose parents ran it until Mrs Cameron died in 1944 when Margaret, who was serving in the W.R.N.S. came home to look after her father and the business until she married and Ewen came home from the navy to join them. Ewen took over and was in the fullness of time joined by his son Angus until the hotel was burned down in 1982.

Four pensioners meet with the Cameron family to celebrate forty years in the Lochearnhead hotel.
Left to right: Cathie Kennedy (Lewis), Joan Mitchell (Lewis), Hamish McGregor (Mull), and Jean Kennedy (Coll). Cathie, Joan and Hamish have all settled in Lochearnhead and all have family near them.

The new chalet complex before landscaping at the new Lochearnhead Hotel. These chalets were shipped from Meilenbourg in Denmark and have proved to be extremely well insulated and warm during the winter when they have a very high occupancy.

This is Granny Kennedy with four of her children at the croft in Glenogle, 1888.

Her eldest son seated on the ground would be Dan who became the father of Donald, Charlie and Gregor, three more boys and six daughters who were so well known in the village.

Sitting on the dyke opposite the shop in 1915. Douglas McLaren (who became the shopkeeper), Christopher McNab, Grace Donald, Willie Thornton and Meg.

Willie Cameron takes his mother-in-law, Mrs Maben for a tour over the hills beyond Killin. 1928.

Lochearnhead school, 1929. From left to right—

Back row: Archie Sinclair, Jimmy McLaren, - MacGregor, - MacGregor, Jock MacGregor, Dick Bryson, Gregor Kennedy, Ian Sinclair, Archie MacGregor.

3rd row: John Lamont, . . . , Jessie Todd, Agnes Todd, Dolly Buchanan, Peggy Kennedy, - MacGregor, Willie Bryson, Alick Buchanan.

2nd row: Christina Kennedy, . . . , Flora MacGregor, Alice MacKinnon, Morag Buchanan, Margaret Cameron, Alasdair Bryson.

Front row: Archie MacKechnie, Donald MacIntosh, Lachie MacKechnie, Sandy Fergusson.

Lochearnhead school, 1931.
   From left to right—
Back row; Alex Fergusson, - Gibson, Hamish MacGregor, John Lamont.
Middle row: Muriel Drummond, Bindy McInnes, Chrissie Kennedy, - Sinclair.
Front row: . . . , Margaret Cameron, Alice MacKinnon, Jean Sinclair Ferguson.

Lochearnhead school, 1960.
    From left to right—
Back row: Alan Saffian, Andrew Bryson, Ronald Morrison, . . . , Philip Hapka, Joe Saffian,
- Campbell, Lachie McGregor.
3rd row: Noretta Mitchell, Mairi Mitchell, . . . , Renee Bryson, Sandra McKenzie,
Moira McKenzie, Isobel Bryson.
2nd row: Jessie Prentice, Shiela Bryson, Moira Kennedy, Lesley Hollington,
Norma McFarlane, Evelyn McKenzie, Jeanette McFarlane, Sandra Geddes, Marie King.
Front row: Willie Bryson, Colin MacLennan, - Campbell, Gordon Campbell,
Stewart Hollington, Neil Kennedy.

Lochearnhead school, 1965. From left to right—
Back row: Stewart & Gordon Cunningham, Patricia & Janet McFarlane, Jesica Prentice, Moira Kennedy, Jeannette Geddes, Allan Prentice, Ian Johnston.
3rd row: Mairi Kennedy, Mike Hopka, Leslie McGregor, Angus Cameron, Christine Murdo Morrison, Neil Kennedy, Angus McDiarmid, Sheena Bryson.
2nd row: Mairi King, Ian Mitchell, Sheena McLachlan, Norma McFarlane, Colin McGregor, Evelyn McKenzie, Sandra Geddes, Catherine McFarlane, Willie Szuszkewicz, Tooti Cameron, Anne Johnston.
Front row: Gillian McLachlan, Fiona McKenzie, Rosemary Brown, John McFarlane, Peter Szuszkewicz, Malcolm MacGregor, John Duncan, Mairia Brown, Allison Geddes, Rhoda McGregor.

The *Queen of Lochearn* berths at Lochearnhead in 1923.

It is welcomed by a piper, a Johnston from Aberfeldy who summered in Lochearnhead. The steamer was run from St Fillans and made two return trips a day during the five summer months. Owned by Alexanders', the bus company from Falkirk, her activities were curtailed by the Board of Trade Regulations after the 39 / 45 war. She gave a wonderful and popular service.

Opposite top
Four well-kent local fiddlers play for a dance at Balquhidder Hall, 1936.
From left to right:
Ronnie Gibson, Hugh MacDiarmid, Jimmy Fergusson, and Constable Sam Allan.

Opposite lower
War in Ethopia and general all round alert in 1936.
The Black Watch on the move through the village and getting the "hello there" from the hotel staff. A large number of local men were in the T.A. which was the Black Watch, and the railways lost many men to the Royal Engineers.

Stewarts of Ardvorlich

The family have been at Ardvorlich on the south side of Lochearn since the mid 1500s. The oldest parts of the present house were built in 1790 and added to in 1890. Sandy and Ginny Stewart and their six children live there to this day.

This is Colonel John Stewart, C.I.E., of Ardvorlich. He was born at Chunar, India and entered the Royal Bengal Artillery in 1857 and during the Mutiny was employed protecting the communications of the Bengal Army in Oudh. He became a Colonel in 1882 and retired to Ardvorlich in 1888.

Opposite top.
The six Kennedy brothers of Glenogle together in 1947.

Left to right:
Donald, Sandy (Canada), Jimmy (Aberfeldy), Charlie (Control Commission, Germany), Neil (Canada) and Gregor at home in Glenogle.

A most popular family in the village and with children and grandchildren still coming and going.

Opposite lower.
The three Kennedy men who remained in Lochearnhead. Donald on the tractor gets his younger brothers Charlie and Gregor organised.

Mr and Mrs McIntyre at Tigh no Hossan opposite the village shop. They lived and worked as a shepherd at Findoglen Ardvorlich before coming into the village where in the middle of this century their family was very

well known, Allan was a joiner and Flora was "the lady in the Post Office" in the days of the McNaughtons and then with Mr and Mrs Davie Sinclair.

Opposite top.
Lochearnhead Drama Club on tour in Muthill, 1929.
From left to right—
Back row: Andrew Dow, Jock McLaren, Jim McLaren.
Middle row: W Macintosh, Jenny McLaren, . . . , Eileen Macgregor, . . . , Alan McIntyre, . . . , . . . , Hugh McDiarmid Snr.
Front row: Mary McLaren, Mr & Mrs Charlie Hunter, Flora McIntyre.

Opposite lower
Lochearnhead Drama Club, 1950.
In *Leaves before the wind* are, from left to right:
Mary Glass, Phemie MacDougall, John Stubbs, Kitty Sinclair and John Reid.

Christopher MacNab, in 1950.
He was the village postie for over forty years.

Opposite top.
Members of the Lochearnhead fire brigade having a practice.
From left to right—
Owen McKee the shop, Denny Maclachlan the postman and Ross Mills the gamekeeper at Glenbeich. The service started in 1961.

Opposite lower.
Lochearnhead country dance team, 1934.
Winners of the Perth Festival that year.
From left to right—
Back row: Jock Reid, Dolly Buchanan, Hamish MacGregor, Jenny McLaren and Hugh MacDiarmid.
Front row: Bunty MacDonald, Wilfred MacDonald and Bella Spy.

Captain Ben Coutts pins the Highland Show Long Service Medal onto Neil Campbell in 1951. Neil had been the cattleman at the hotel since 1918. He was born on the Island of Coll and when he came to Lochearnhead he only spoke Gaelic.

The Prime Minister of Australia, Sir Robert Menzies and Dame Pattie Menzies, at the local Gathering.

The Chieftain and the President in conference, 1955.

Sir Gregor MacGregor of MacGregor, Bt. and Jimmy Ferguson, Muirlaggan.

Lochearnhead Games in 1964.
Sir Alec Douglas Hume arrives with the President, Jimmy Fergusson, Muirlaggan and the Secretary, Ewen Cameron.

The Games, 1966.
The Chieftain, Captain Watters Macrae, Edinample with Lady Douglas Home.

The Committee of the B.L.&S. Highland Games gathers on the morning of the 1993 Gathering.
From left to right: James Stewart, Roy Gauld, John Lawrie, Roger Sharpe, Kate McInally, Angus Cameron, Liz Wishart, Olive & Lottie Cameron, Ewen & Anne Cameron, Tommy Anderson, Jim Heron, Ian Robertson, Charlie Meikle, Kenny McCallum, Lennox Jamieson, Stan Collingwood, Mary McCallum, Jim McGrandles, Dennis Ramsay, Charlie Methven.

A gathering for Tom Lambie's retirement party.

Tom was a well-known shepherd in Glenogle for many years. Davie McDiarmid, Tom and Dochie Stewart.

The opening March, 1987.
Left to right: Derek Hunnisett, Chieftain; Robert Gibbons, Vice President; Donald McLaren of McLaren; The Macnab of Macnab; Ewen Cameron, President.

Edinchip curlers on Loch Lubnaig, 1949.
From left to right: Duncan McIntyre, Stroneslaney, Pat Palmer (now General Sir Patrick Palmer of the Argyll & Sutherlands and Governor of Windsor Castle), Major Crawford Dunlop, Ronnie Gibson of Strathyre Garage, Bill King of Kingshouse Hotel, Major Jock Stewart of Ardvorlich and Jimmy Hogan from Stronvar Gardens.

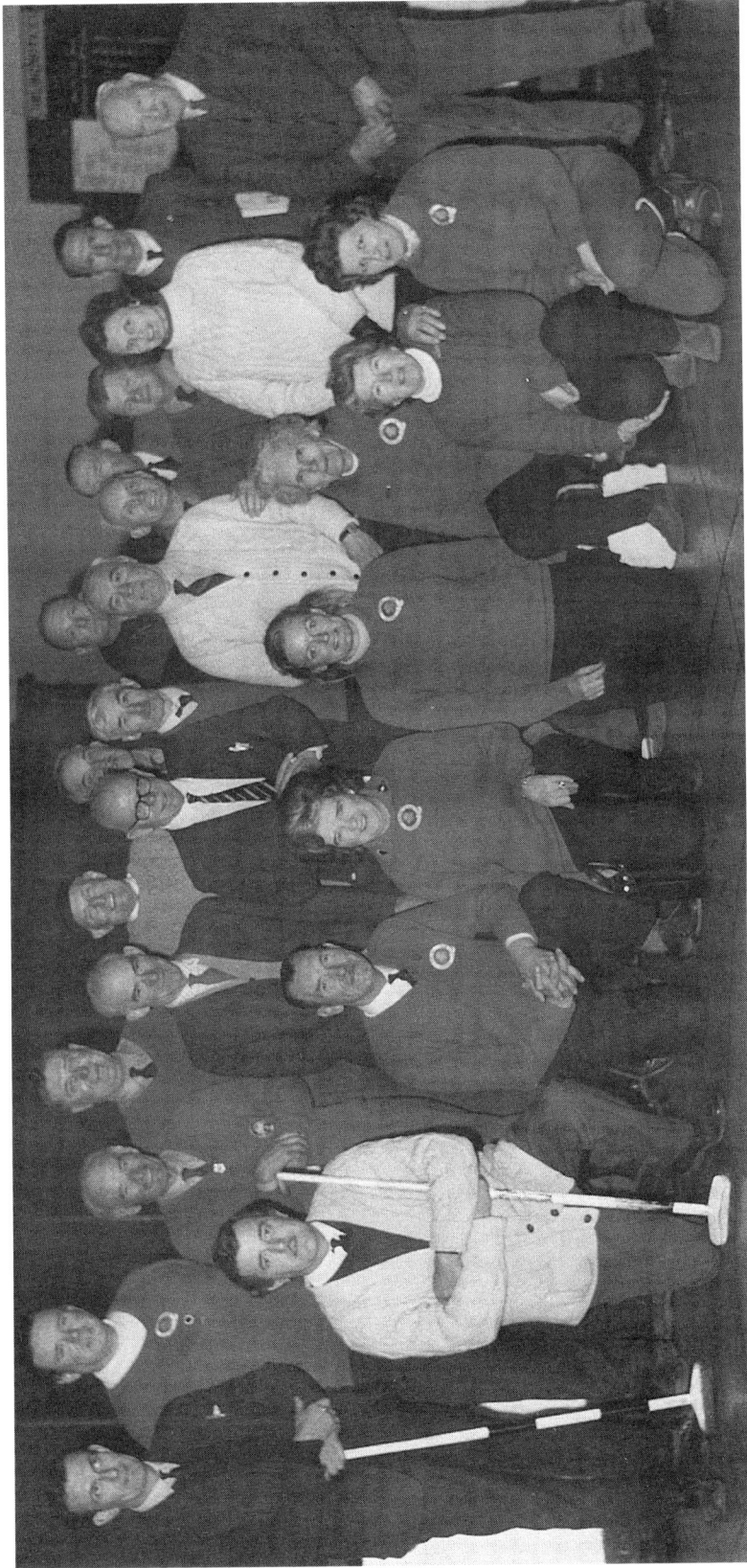

A club outing for the Edinchip Curling Club in 1971.

They hailed from all three villages in the parish and one or two from further afield. Their main ice rink was Perth but in good frost the Edinchip pond was their home. In really severe winters Lochs Lubnaig and Voil heard the roar of their stones. The Club was founded in 1870 and by 1872 they were playing for a Caledonian Medal against Comrie, expenses of the players to be paid for by the club. Unfortunately the Club after many happy years came to a slow ending due to old age of the stalwart members and the Breathalyser. The young people talk of a comeback – we hope so and wish them well.

From left to right:

Back row: Tommy McGregor, Ewen Camero, Jack Scott, Bob Davidson, Andrew Waugh, Donald Kennedy, Lewis Drysdale, Tom Lambie, J. C. Fergusson, Donald Steele, Duncan Clark, Alex McCrae, Sandy Scott, Alf Cunningham, Chris Foster, Ronald Gibson, Davie Sinclair.

Front row: Hamish McGregor, Charlie Lunn, Margaret Waugh, Anne Cameron, Briget Hamilton-Smith, Winifred Kelly, Irene Brown.

Lochearnhead Junior Badminton Club. Formed in 1980, it unfortunately came to an untimely end with the building of the New Hall which was not high enough to allow play.
From left to right
Back Row: Rhoda McGregor, Pauline Reilly, Doreen McKinnon-Taylor,
Second Row: Raymond Baines, Alistair McSkimming, Fiona McKee, Douglas McLaughlan, Jennifer Veitch, ...
Front row: Andrew Baynes, Callum Millls, Fiona Bowers, Roddy McKee, Alison Perks, Debbie Anderson, Fiona Perks, Mhairie McKee.

Hamish McGregor with a stag shot in Edinchip in 1978.

Hamish, who learned his trade at Fassifern near Corpach, came to Edinchip where his father was manager to Sir Malcolm MacGregor the Clan Chieftain. He has now been over forty years with the Camerons, switching happily between the bar of the hotel and Glenogle farm and is certainly one of the best known figures in the area. Now he looks after the Glenogle herd of Highland cattle.